Every Sunrise

Title: Every Sunrise / Cameron Hindrum
ISBN 9780645089394
Front cover image credit: 'Gravity's Veil' (detail), (c) 2022 Martin Cole. Acrylic on board. Used by permission of the artist.
Back cover image credit: S Group/Richard Harmey

Walleah Press
South Launceston
Tasmania, Australia 7249

www.walleahpress.com.au
ralph.wessman@walleahpress.com.au

Every Sunrise

Cameron Hindrum

Nothing now but the bookmark of a horizon.

You grip my little finger tightly.

...

We are as pure and strange as Sanskrit words.

We greet the sun, whom we resemble.

Marjana Savka,
from 'Books we've never read'

Translated from Ukrainian
by Askold Melnyczuk

CONTENTS

DAWN

DAY

This, and everything within and around:

for Sonja.

Dawn

Table Cape

Young, fishing with my father,
slicing open wide odyssean water,
shadow rising of the cold volcano:
impenetrable coffin-black rocks,
vast and monolithic,
a sheer smooth-sided plug

that had once contained all measure
of Earth's
powerful violence.

                                         But now

I am merely cradled
on the ocean, setting nets,
waiting for fish, with
the half-sweet Port Royal fug
from my father's rollie
caught on the sweat

of the sea.

The Bird You Are

For Gerri

For a long time
there were only sips of something,
whispered at:

how cruel it seemed,
in that house of tired love,
which had always bristled with
you, your sharp tongue now
softened, and accepting
only bird-like morsels.

How the sky deflates
and draws itself in
as days become grey
and difficult to distinguish
one from another.

But in the room
that became you
you accepted food like
a lovely bird,

with all the sky
to behold.

On Collins Street, Hobart, 7am

This place of glass and silence
early-morning-solemn

                              empty

waits for better sunlight, and
the soak of noise
        from another day.

Where shadows are not yet born,
everything is closed up

                        into stillness

breath held.

A man, escaped from sleep,
alone near the shoe shop,
yells at the empty world:
a conversation

only he

understands.

Prostitute! Slut! Yeah
Fuckin run away
Gutless bitch!
Fuckin prostitute! Run!

Away from him,
I cross the street. I stare
into silent shops, trying
to find a place for him
and failing.

Some new
                    meaning

nowhere to be found.

Eventually, he too
is quiet;
but by then

I have turned away,
wondering which
one of us

                                        is alone.

At Storys Creek

Except for the ghosts of houses,
    an abandoned town
    has no memory:

this is where footprints
    of man and building
    dissolve into gathering ground.

An absent river, blighted
    within banks of rust
    carries poison-weighted water

away from the rain off the distant bluff.

Rain is merciful here: it is not weeping
    for open wounds, lost
    fortunes, or faded lives;

the pillagers are gone, having reaped
    what they could, leaving
    nothing to sow or to be sown.

And so the rain bleeds gently
    into a wounded earth
    through piled waste

and taints itself.

Below the scars and wounds and waste,
    bad water in a blighted river
    watches the only sky.

Lunch with My Daughter
at the Age of Eight

Those innocent eyes
survey the street:
I wonder what shapes
they see.

She is not yet
at the age of
important questioning;

the world for her
is blank
and colourful.

She finishes sushi
leaning into me, her head
an invisible weight
upon my shoulder.
I breathe her in,
this ghost of me,
this unformed promise
of everything.
I wonder where
her fears will emerge
and when
she will start
losing sleep.

I cannot hold for her.

I cannot make
many things okay.
I have only hope,
that vast membrane
against
the rest of her life.

I will not count
moments like this one,
but keep them instead
as a fragment of time when
there were no questions.

There are yet windows between
her
and the vast ephemeral world,
the one she observes
like television.

I watch her. I slow
down time
and try
not to listen

to my fears.

After Aubade

I drove home against the phone call
While your breath was slowly losing
        Its punctuation.

Pale bloodless early light
chasing the sun towards the sky
tendril smoke menthol fresh bending
Reaches for unformed shadows,
unwinding
ribboning through that icy window crack
Crafting the doubt of another day:
Planning the conversation
twisting my fear into unknown shapes
I cannot finish, except in my promises.

Cigarettes help the road unfold
And give me something else to think about,
Other than
        Your breathing
Slowly losing
        Its punctuation

A siren paralyses at 4am
Screaming under sunrise, slicing
Open sleep: withdrawn darkness
Driving home against the phone call
        Unwinding

Pale bloodless early light
tendril smoke menthol fresh bending
Reaching for unformed shadows
chasing the sun towards the sky
twisting my fear into unknowable shapes
Crafting the doubt of another day.

In transit, invisible city.
Invisible rhythms, slowing, quiet.
In pale, bloodless early light

My fear is twisted
into the shape of
your unpunctuated breathing,
                        unwinding.

Promise/Absence

I leave my house and its
warmth and get into my car.
I hope that it starts first
time. My car is like a tired
 old man who still wants to
be useful—sometimes it's
capable and sometimes it
isn't, but you keep it around
because it's full of stories. I
remember going to see my
great-grandmother when I
was a child, and she thought
my father was still a
fisherman even though at
that point he had not been
near the water for very
many years. He would
return to the water long
after she died. In her old
room, my great
grandmother smelled like
soap; she reminded me of
flowers long kept in a vase
that still hold their shape,
flowers with a quiet ghostly
scent that remain beautiful
 when they are dead.

I start the car and the old
man listens and my great-
grandmother is sitting next
to me, holding flowers in her
papery hands. The flowers
are growing and eventually
they fully occupy the interior
of the car. Their scent is
what fills me from within,
lighter than air. The car is
still moving but the door
opens and I am lifted up and
out, and there is all the sky.

I think about this as I drift
calmly over the Southern
Outlet. And I think that
soon I will buy my wife
some young flowers, crisp
with absent promise.

Oceans

I have this black and sacred book
spanning the years like an ocean.

Inside it, I cast a look
at ideas all set in tidal motion
drifting out on ebbs of suggestion,
when each day opens like a question.
This is the vessel of my want,
the assembled trove of all my fears.

The treasured source of all détente,
when the Muse offers nothing and sneers.
These are my words, yet tied to shore –
unless I can make of them something more.
I adore this chaos, this disorder:
this revelation that oceans *have no border.*

Three Poems About My Funeral That I Will Never Read

"Literature (is) the only possible resurrection, outside heaven and hell."

Barry Dickins

i

When I die
I want to become
a note, sung
in single harmony
lifted on breath
and held
without
reverberation

ii

Do not hold
my funeral
inside.

Do not play
the wrong music,
but do not
let there be
silence.
Do not cry too loudly—

I am intent
on the next bit. And
most importantly
after the flames
keep me with you until
you too
are ready.

iii

I will seek
in gorgeous nebula,
a swift-hearted
no-sided shifting
ash shadow
that I could not find

in the firmament.

Closer to Heaven

She quietly opens herself.
Tired bliss tugs at the corners
of her mouth.
She draws blood like it's nothing,
like taking a step, like swallowing.
Like a flower, she opens herself
peeling back the petal
of her faded pink hoodie.
She's taking it
in the neck this time,
the waiting vein like a vine,
curling itself around her, waiting
while she draws blood without blinking
wondering why it takes longer
for the drugs to work
and why's she so tired
of opening herself
to a dying sun.

Untitled Poem for Home

Upon the occasion of a high school reunion, 2013

I have wondered now for an unknown hour
how I would make it home
how I would find you, everyone, waiting
for time to shift its mirror:

I wondered how we would survive
the slow-motion sprint of memory:
the urge to find you again, and smile
and say hello, and mean it.

We assemble here, for a moment
in time, in the shadow of every ghost:
cradled in the curve of a cold volcano
listening to ourselves as we were -

younger

and hungry, then, for anything.

Time is not the enemy here: we
become our own rhythm, measured
by the patient tide. We patrol
that border, between the land
and the sea, and we leave
our ghosts behind, in the soft
give of the sand:

water will erase our evidence:

and yet we will walk

again, still.

Haircut

Nine-year-old me
peeks out from under the fringe
steps out of the mirror
walks down the street
through years
of Saturday mornings, by
silent water, the air
unwarmed and breathable.

Nine-year-old me had
straight edges
big blue eyes
watching the shy man
cut his hair.

He waits, that boy,
in shadowed corners
for time to at least
slow down: stopping altogether
is too much to ask.

No one cuts his hair now.

The Bridge, January 5, 1975

For my father

i.
Something quiet punched a hole in the road
across water: in near darkness,

                                no one saw it coming.

The cleft in the great wide night-mouth
yawned under evening traffic,

as wide

and as deep

as history.

ii.

People fell: in cars now graceless
with gravity, unflighted like drunken birds,
diving through dreams
                        darker than water,

a criminal current
washing over grave
mistakes,
                the doubt

more deadly than a hard nudge:
starboard against cement.

Before there had been the only way home,
now there was an edge:
                                  sudden-sliced,
                                              silent.

iii.

Watch the curving spine ascend
and return with equal grace
to earth: its vertebrae stand erect,
proud over poisonous water: watch
the silent eddies lap abutments,
falling and receding.
The thousand vessels,
the thousand cars,
the thousand turns of sun: watch
the simple act of passage, time
and time, and time again.

iv.

Remember bloody Des Kelly? Cocky bugger,
chugging beers as the ferry chugged
under the lightless gap.

Des, the bloody champion
making the crossing, Hobart to Bellerive
in ten 10-ounce beers

and a seven-minute piss.

Days truncated, as working men measured
the line between shores
in empty glasses.

v.

Across the bodies
where water meets water

and no one talks   *about the bridge*

vi.

We pulled him from the yawning dark, oil-slicked
and bloodworn, drenched
in diesel and the smell of fear,

sodden through
and lost in the darkness of losing his ground,

cold and coughing to raise the dead, folded
in the corner of the wheelhouse.

We said, *fuckin what happened mate,*

where'd the bloody boat go?   And he said

she's gone, cut by the road across the bow,
down like a poor man's puddin she went. Fuckin

fifteen minutes it took.

Any a youse blokes got a smoke?

vii.

East and west are meaningless
in the great scheme of things.
There is no homeward turn,
away from metaphor:
there is only the promise of being home
crossing the benign bridge
that great homeward arc:
that intersection of here and elsewhere,
of what is important and not. It withstands
the power of the tide to turn
the vastness of a vessel against itself.

Look upon that infinite cleft   and let it

remind you: nothing can be promised.

viii.

One car we never found. Might be
crushed under the roadway
that fell across the *Illawarra's* bow

but we never found it. Only a strip of chrome:
six, seven inches, twisted.

All that was left
of the journey
                                    home.

ix.

The tide will always come.
The remembering,

>   *skin like old ash, eyes*
>   *rollin back in his head like marbles.*

The garage door
closed, everyone
safe where they should be
and warm

>   *the roll of the river*
>   *cradling us*
>   *as if to sleep.*

Twilight
lending its meeting place:
what is, what has been.

Every Sunrise

A poem

defines
space

between its promise
and you:
small words

such a vast space

Morning:
sheets of soft pink
are thrown
like
                    stories
over the day

Measure the hours
you have;

don't count them…

At Port Arthur
I told ghost stories
in the ghosts
        of buildings.

On most nights,
the moon winked
        over my shoulder

As a child
I walked by
the river, by
the jetty
where boats waited.

The tide went
out and in
but the boats
never seemed

to leave.

Peace is
the open vowel
of an endless aria:

the space into which
you love against

everything

A footprint
is a map

behind me
a line of them
stretches away

tattooed
on the skin
of the sand

I drove home
against the phone call
chasing the sun
towards the sky
tendril smoke
menthol fresh
bending my fear
into shapes
of cold

          A distant siren
            reminds me
        what hope is for

When I was young
my father
bowled to me
looping
            off-spinners
in the park
near our house:

now,
returning –
parked cars
field at short leg

Waking to
the staccato
of birdsong

morning
percussion

diamond
syllables

an invisible
sound
of home

Everything was infinite
when I was younger
but I am no longer
of a mountain made—

One winter
the snow came
and locked
the land
in white;

we drove
blind
through the cloud
through crowded

emptiness

Waiting for you
a lone seagull
mocks traffic

In the line
that enlarges
out of the horizon,
every sunrise

is every birth

The streets
are awash
with the ghost
of rain

Careful billowing sorrow,
spider-web delicate,
      strong
      with the gift
of ages

To teach me
how to swim
my father
carried
me out, past
my depth
and dropped me:

I thrashed,
but eventually
found a rhythm.

The ocean
welcomes
me, still

If you stand
long enough
at the edge
of a river

in time

you'll find
the echo
of its rhythms
in your own

Early sky
like charcoal,
barely cold
embers:
the warmth
of sleep

Rich are the gifts
of waiting
when the day
opens

like a question

At twilight,
birds
like flicks
of ink
punctuate

sunset

As the sky
darkens,
trees
with branches
like a thousand
fingers reach
gently

for each other

New leaves
offer an invitation:

begin

The endless hour
drifting
between awake and arise:

afloat
before any harm
behind half-open eyes

Three truths:

oceans have no border
the sun, too, will die;
my words will

outlive me

                                    The day after
                                      your birth
                                         the sun
                                   shone harder
                                   on my fears

fire
heart
sleep

and

            [there is
                  no poem
            here   ]

In Spring
even the sun
seems
      cleaner

                                        A leaf
                                    is a map

                                    of perfect
                              intersections

                                  from which
                        we should learn

A beach
is a line
between land
and sea
as old
as symmetry

The chill
of the morning
running
silver

through the river's
shadows: again

this waking
world

Under the fragile lights
the music hides secrets;

But still
he will hold her

Peace is
the weight
of sleep:
warm morning

Summer is when
days begin
in the middle
and last
a week

Walking
is breathing
light,
a moment when

the mind
rehearses
the rest of the day

Art should
with great affection
flood the streets

and drown us all

If only
I could inhale
the colours
of a sunrise
and save them

Monday morning
is the weight
of wishing
I was unemployed

Autumn is
soft, slow change:

a sleepening

Home is merely
the heart
broken open

Day

The Hazara

Hold a child's hand,
and never feel fear again:
they have felt all the fear
in the world.

How we must always be welcoming
how open our eyes
and hearts
must always be
to their belonging.

Love speaks no other language
than the holding of a hand,
the joy of running in open air
playing in places of no danger:

this is the freedom that we must give.
Dismantling generations of doubt
with the passage of a smile, and
the holding out

                    of a hand.

I Don't Know What to Tell You About Your Poems

I don't know what to say
                about your poems.
I mean, they're beautiful, and
they break my heart
in illuminating ways –
but I don't know
                what to say.

I left them on the page and I walked
for a while into myself,
searching empty places
for non-repeating echoes,
listening for answers I don't have.

That's, I think, how I felt as I walked
into the aching cavern
of your words, you
asking of me a faith
by which the shapes of the poems
would rise against
mere gravity.

They stand, these gentle poems of yours,
with their light and their
shifting shadows,
though there is so much
unspoken. I could hear

their silence
a thousand times –
and still not know

        what to say.

Weeping humbly, as you have wept,
is of course too little.

There is not, perhaps, enough doubt
in the world; yet I am powerless
to make any more. So while I cannot
say what it is you must be told –
while I cannot forge a compass
that might show you the way, I can

        perhaps

give you only this:

write more poems.

As lonely as the world
may sometimes seem
it will only be more lonely

        without them.

After Bit.Fall

Standing underground,
four ceilings deep, and vaulted:
formless water words
shuffle unsurprising headlines
marking invisible news with
gravity-fed ghost words
syncing rhythm
with the ghosts
of ideas:
this sound
will fade over time,
dissolving even
the news,

even the stone underground heart

of the truth.

The Light and the Empty Lane

Notice, will you, how she dives into
the water. How angular and slight the
sun makes her, against itself. How she
is gone for a moment, swallowed in
light while the world is silent. Water
moves out of the way for her. Notice
how, a perfect machine, she reappears
and pulls herself along. How she
rejoices, how she is now a metronome,
her arms keeping time against the
clock. The early sun also welcomes
her with diamonds, casting them
light-flecked in her path. Notice how
they roll over her, her back and her
legs, tracing her with their own
beauty before they vanish.

If only the water would drain away,
leaving her transfixed in the air in her
strength: that too would be beautiful.
If only she would be challenged by
nothing more than having to make it
to the wall, and then tumble through
herself and push off again, repeating
and resisting. If only she could learn
to exist outside time, outside
expectation. I want nothing more for
her than this.

But there will always be time, and
there will always be water and I hope
there will always be the poetry of
grace as she makes her way through
it, carving up sunlight, racing time to
one end and then the other, over and
over again. There will always be time
dividing the length of days into laps,
into metres of laps, into moments.
There will always be early sunlight,
making tomorrow and yesterday.

There will always, I hope, be me—
sitting with a forgotten book, away
from the water, watching her and not
being anywhere.

An Ode to PCs Dagg and Shayler

It wasn't a normal day at work
for members of the constabulary
but there you were, clean shaven and stiff,
trying to stop the Beatles.

While the melodious strains of Get Back
rained gently on the shoppers of London
30 complaints in 30 minutes
spurred you two into action.

It's possible you probably weren't expecting
the greatest rock band in the world
to ruin your lunch hour -- but then,
as they say in fracture clinics, thems the breaks.

And up to the roof you bravely ventured
into the cauldron of popular culture
and stood there, staring blankly while John
(still a decade from death) dug his pony.

To be fair, you probably didn't know
because no one did in that shining moment
that they would never play live again –
but that didn't stop you. It had to be stopped

because the pretty white people of London
complained, and all things considered, when
complaints start rolling in -- well,
you can't just let it be.

But in the end, popular culture bows
to no man. Your bobbys' shields
couldn't stop the music, and the Beatles
passed the audition. As they were always going to.

The band broke up not long afterwards
(and not because anyone complained)
while you two were probably
still busy with the paperwork.

Blockies

Yeeeeeah mate
life is a circle, don't they tell ya
an endless Friday night
in the green HR panno
embraced by cracked vinyl, incense
(that's what we tell the cops it is)
lighting our way out of work
into getting shitfaced, forgetting
how hard work is to come by
living day to every other day.

Cops never believe us.

Got no cash for nightlife, got no
place to be, home is someone's couch
most nights.

Gun it at the O'Keefe's Corner lights:
stare down the dickhead in the 120Y
slip the clutch a second early, whip it:
Yeeeeeeeeah!
Sing that endless Goodyear squeal,

nothin like it in the world, mate.

Drifting in a circle, waiting
for the next Friday night. Happy
as pigs in shit, mate. That's what

it's all about.

Yellow Lines

That was us, running.

It was dark and after the eating. They were all standing around, beers and all, laughing, talking shit. Don't know what time.

We were in the big yard at the back of the station when we heard it. The Christmas barbie, the volunteers and families and kids, the two full-time blokes. They moved the two big red tankers to make room, out on the street with the little bushie tucked up behind one of them like a patient puppy. Us kids were playing a half-arsed game of cricket out the back under the floodlight from the corner of the roof.

Can't describe the sound. Tyres locked up, a squeal harsh in the darkness, a soft crump, metal hitting metal like a full stop at the end of the squealing and glass breaking. We all looked around, at each other and out to the street. Someone's droppin doughies, Ginger said, and Towel hissed back, shut up Ginger. The way there was the long desperate scream of the tyres and then the thud and then nothing. Fuck me, we all froze. Just for a moment.

Ginger was batting and ran first, back through the shed and down the wide driveway out onto the street. Didn't take long for the adults to cotton on and by then we were all running, them trying to catch up. Someone yelling, fuckin stop em!

But they didn't. Eighty or a hundred metres up the street, back towards the shops. Little dark white flatbed truck had pulled out in front of a motorbike, had two blokes on it. Slammed into the cabin. One of them was across the other side of the street, looked like he was hugging a tree and the other one was hanging from the shattered window of the truck by an arm. There was blood and oil and glass and stuff all over the road. I could see it in the poor white streetlight. Nothing moved. Silent night.

Stark on the dark road,
passed over blindly:
soft lines, hazard-yellow
curl against the sun:

an accident here, they say,
showing you the point
of impact and rest, time
and motion, movement,
stillness, terminus.

All that's left are these
yellow lines, imprinted
on the road: poor graffiti,
poorer warning, the news
of someone not coming

home. I pass over them,
thinking about teaching
my son to drive, hoping
it will make a difference:

and where broken
the broken fellow lay,
the lines seem to converge,
and say: Do not turn away.

Look. You must look. And
always take care.

Lake Poems

i.

You drift against ghost gum calligraphy
borne on silence, the twilight
hour that lasts all day,
coming in ancient morning
standing alone without reflection.
Some measure of eternity
sculpts stillness out of sun,
drifting like bluest smoke,
across placid, passive water,
into the texture of the trees.

ii
Out of silvered quiet
morning rises, breaking
ice-edged surfaces
into exact pieces,
caught before melting...

Comes the canvas of the endless day
cast between a frame of trees
painted with the joy
of forgetting time,
the sky shifting, darkening
reflected in patchwork mirror,
braced in breeze and the whisper
of unvacant country
before gunshot and gentry
claimed the kingdom of the visible.

But now

serrated duck wings percuss the water
making the only violence
scattering the perfect surface into
fragments of history, which drift towards
a distant edge,
never to meet.

Untitled Poem About My Cat

Where soft the mocking shadow
falls against dismembered line
dark against dark against dark
she makes the night time
part of herself, at one with the idea
of negative   space.

Apostrophic, unannounced
the suggestion of weight
is here and now in the lightening space
between daylight and waking:
not affection as we know it, but its
shadowed ghost, the suggestion of love,
like an unwritten letter.

Breathing is Nothing
in the Context
of the Universe

IM Bec Phillips

It is not possible. There is no
understanding. There is no right by
which the sun can shine on such a
day, while you lay in silence cloud-
wrapped and waiting, and earth is
returned to you. How does life look
when interrupted? When birds will
not truncate their song or leaves will
not suspend themselves in the air?

How is it possible for the heat of the
sun to still reach my skin on such a
lonely day?

There can be no dream any more, no
light of possibility. I know you would
not like me to think so. Breathing is
nothing in the context of the
universe—a futile, shallow thing. It
does not help. It keeps nothing away.
There is simply too much of
everything.

Now we turn away from the moment,
looking to make sense. There is no
sense to be made, even less than there
is understanding to be found.
Everything eventually burns, we all
know this.

We return
to that
from which
we came.

We are cycles, an endless loop of
stuff, given shape and momentum and
reduced again when the cycle must
repeat itself. There is no comfort in
this. It is how we are made.

Are we left with a collection of
ghosts, of exquisite things that we
cannot touch, of places we will never
be? Perhaps therein lies the beauty of
the bloody moment: that we can
shroud ourselves against
understanding.

Perhaps there will come acceptance,
or something like it. Something close
enough. Something.

Cusp

For Gemima

i.
Draw a line slowly
to the centre of the page
and find out how strong
the centre is:
it will hold.

Yeats was wrong.

Draw a line, outwards
to the edge of everything:
      and live there, too.

ii
An ocean's waves
will always return:
the same water.

Every time.

iii.
We are all wise
watching a sunrise
when the day is still slow
and we know what we know.

What we don't know is where
on lifted currents of unseen air
we will be carried; or what
we will know
instead of Knowing.

Two Haiku

Morning swim:
how soon
the water forgets me

Cold air
braces trees against
unframed sky

Fire Season

Crafted like wind
the shape of angry time, an
ache of our history:
it possesses
without ownership.

The distant tendrils
obey the laws of breath
and ghost themselves:

in more fecund ways, they flood
                                by flicker and leaping reach,
mocking ancient gums.

Unfettered,
                        cloud-curled
claw-edged
                                    rushing empty,
dissolving memory,
                                    solid and not.

                    Soft colours rise
                from the floor of dark hues
                    in newborn silence

when futility has faded
    and, on our behalf,
    the landscape
    is rendered

                                    blank, again.

What I Wanted to Tell You

My eyes are not as a woman's eyes...
John Shaw Neilsen, 'The Loving Tree'

I was told not to go near the house of the old woman,
tucked away from earth behind the thick line of trees at
the old end of town. The town of my childhood is not the
town you know today. The things that made it rich are
gone. Silent people live there now.

But this is not what I wanted to tell you. One cold
afternoon I defied my parents, as all children eventually
do, and walked towards that end of town. I wanted to see
the old woman. Why should I be kept from her? Mother
and Father had strange ideas but I wanted to see for
myself. Under the sky that afternoon, I walked towards
her.

The line of trees had been planted too close together, not
long after the war. You might never have known a house
was there. You could see nothing of it from the town
road. Just trees, vast sentinel things now, silent and close
to each other, trying to reach the clouds.

I walked towards them carefully, as if they might shift
and start reaching for me. Giant things. I remember the
soft grass under my sandals, cushioning me from
unknown earth. The grass was long and I could feel its
icy fingers scratching at the skin of my calves, reaching
for the hem of my long skirt. One of Mother's creations.

The leather straps of my sandals were soon wet, sliding against my feet like polished glass. I took careful steps, many of them, wondering whether I should be counting, watching the waiting trees. I felt, finally, the voice of the old woman.

Come. Let me see you.

Beyond the trees, there was no house.

On Going to Visit
My Father in his 83rd Year
and Finding Him Asleep

Yes, there is
the shallow curve
of breath. No other shape
in the too-small room,
where even the
obscene neon
sincerity
of the
television
game show is
muted, under the
shallow curve of your breath.

Once, those lungs (that pulsate
softly now) knew the might
of a brick wall southerly.
There was nothing quiet
about the gales that
would come
against
your youth.

This silence now
seems an unfair prize
for you, whose multitudes
contain multitudes, whose

memories are now
breathing on
their own
in a box
in the
back bedroom.

I stand there.
I clear away what's left
of what you had for lunch: prawns,
shells carefully sucked, their fragile
broken bodies wrapped in paper.
Forgotten. I watch your
harmless, pallid
breathing, while outside
it rains politely, promising
more in a way that I
cannot.

For a tiny instant,
there is nothing else
in the world
for me, but
that shallow

rise and fall,
rise and
fall.
Not quite
invisible.
Completely
silent.

The rain
whispers
against
the world:
the tide
goes in
and out,
the television
speaks
to no one,

and I
will come
again
tomorrow
until

there

are

no

more.

Arohanui

A word bridges the unknowable water,
Called upon from other islands,
from hearts
similar to ours
and beautifully different:

where soft open syllables fall,
there may be forgiveness
and humility, something like
a kind of hope beyond mortal dreams:

Arohanui.

In sickness
in being still
and in death.

What will survive of us is love, say the poets.

On this island, in this place
we will always be lucky
if this is all that matters.

For in this place of
idle thoughts
and old geology,
hope can ever prosper:
in the only place
that has ever truly
felt like home.

Notes

'Closer to Heaven' is inspired by the photographic portrait, by Molly Harris, of the same name. It can be viewed at the link below but discretion is advised: the image may be confronting to some.

https://www.portrait.gov.au/npppphoto/18068/.

The Bridge, January 5, 1975: At about 9pm on Sunday, January 5, 1975, the 7000-ton bulk ore carrier *Lake Illawarra* drifted off course while navigating the Derwent River through Hobart in southern Tasmania, and collided with several pylons of what was then the only bridge that carried traffic across the river between the two major sections of the city. Three bridge spans and a 127-metre section of roadway collapsed into the river and onto the bow of the tanker, which sank; several cars drove off the resulting gap and in total 12 people lost their lives (seven on the *Lake Illawarra*, and five in cars).

After Bit.Fall: Julius Popp, artist; exhibited at MONA, Tasmania.

An Ode to PCs Dagg and Shayler was written after viewing the excellent Peter Jackson documentary, *Get Back*.

'Arohanui' is a Maori greeting which broadly translates as 'with great affection'.

Acknowledgements

The Hazara, Table Cape, Blockies and Arohanui originally formed part of a sequence, *The Island Song Cycle*, which was developed in conjunction with Ryan Beeton-Binns (tenor), and Emily Sanzaro (harp) for the 2019 Junction Arts Festival. The poems formed spoken-word interludes within the larger performance.

The sequence of poems Every Sunrise was developed as part of a project, 'InstaPoems', for the 2017 Junction Arts Festival.

I am enormously grateful to the Junction Arts Festival for both of these opportunities and for its ongoing support of The Arts in Tasmania.

'After Aubade' was commissioned and performed (as 'Letter to Mother') for the 2023 ECHO Festival, Swansea, Tasmania. My thanks to Young Dawkins and Ange Boxall for this opportunity.

The poems The Bird You Are, Untitled Poem for my Cat, At Storys Creek and the verse section of Yellow Lines were originally published in *Dancing the Light*, edited by Jaydeep Sarangi and Robert Harle, Cyberwit, 2020.

I am indebted to DC Chambial for his friendship in poetry over the last few years, and for the opportunity to publish a selection of my poems in *Poetcrit*.

Promise/Absence, What I Wanted to Tell You and the prose section of Yellow Lines were published in slightly different form by *Island Magazine Online*. My enormous thanks to Ben Walter for his editorial insight and advice.

For their wonderful wisdom and guidance as I embarked on the journey of collecting and editing this volume, I am vastly grateful to Kristen Lang and Tim Slade.

CH